second Position

Preparatory studies

for the cello

by Cassia Harvey

CHP290

www.charveypublications.com - print books
www.learnstrings.com - PDF downloadable books
www.harveystringarrangements.com - chamber music

Study Notes

1. Keep each finger curved as you shift with it.
2. Stay in each position until a finger number tells you to shift to a new position.
3. **Finger charts** for the second position notes that are studied in this volume are located at the back of the book.

1. Shifting to C♯ from 1st Finger

Cassia Harvey

Au Claire de la Lune

Trad., arr. Harvey

2. Playing 2nd Finger D

French Dance

Trad., arr. Harvey

3. Playing C♯, D, and E in Second Position

The Fly Has Married the Bumblebee

Trad., arr. Harvey

4. Learning 3rd Finger D♯

By Our Gates

Trad., arr. Harvey

5. Playing 3rd Finger D#

Miss Mary Mack

Trad., arr. Harvey

6. Shifting Back from 2nd Finger

Dance

Praetorious, arr. Harvey

F#, C#
G#

7. Shifting to 2nd Finger

Frog in the Pool

Trad., arr. Harvey

F#, C#
G#

8. Skipping Notes in Second Position

When I Was a Cobbler

Trad., arr. Harvey

F#, C#
G#

9. Shifting back to B from 4th Finger

White Dove

Trad., arr. Harvey

10. Mixing 2nd and 3rd Fingers

Trad., arr. Harvey

Cuckoo's Nest

Trad., arr. Harvey

11. Shifting to E from 1st Finger

The Staines Morris Tune

Trad., arr. Harvey

12. A String Second Position Review

Russian Folk Song

Tchaikovsky, arr. Harvey

13. Second Position on the D String: F#

Cotton-Eyed Joe

Trad., Harvey

14. Learning F♯ and G

A-Hunting We Will Go

F♯, C♯

Trad., Harvey

15. 4th Finger A

Shoemaker's Dance

Trad., arr. Harvey

F♯, C♯

16. Second Position Workout

Gallop

Trad., Harvey

F#, C#

17. 3rd Finger G#

Hey, Betty Martin

Trad., Harvey

18. More 3rd Finger G♯

German Folk Song

Trad., Harvey

19. Shifting Back from 2nd Finger

Oh, Susanna

Foster, arr. Harvey

20. 2nd Finger Shifting Study

German Folk Dance

Trad., arr. Harvey

F#, C#

©2016 C. Harvey Publications All Rights Reserved.

21. Shifting Back from 4th Finger

Minuet

Bach, arr. Harvey

22. Shifting Up to 4th Finger A

Little Silver Moon

Trad., arr. Harvey

23. Mixing 2nd and 3rd Fingers

Marcio Gallop

Trad., Harvey

24. G and G♯ in Second Position

Botany Bay

Trad., arr. Harvey

F♯, C♯

25. Shifting to B on the G String

Rigadoon

Purcell, arr. Harvey

26. 4th Finger D on the G String

Acadian Lullaby

Trad., arr. Harvey

F#, C#

27. Playing 3rd Finger C♯

Country Gardens

Trad., arr. Harvey

28. C♯ Study

Oh Kumko, Borrow Barrels

Trad., arr. Harvey

29. Shifting Between 1st and 2nd Fingers

Cuckoo

Trad., arr. Harvey

30. Shifting Between 1st and 4th Fingers

All the Pretty Little Horses

Trad., arr. Harvey

31. Shifting to E on the C String

French-Canadian Folk Song

Trad., arr. Harvey

32. Finger Exercise

Russian Wedding Song

Trad., arr. Harvey

33. Learning 3rd Finger F♯

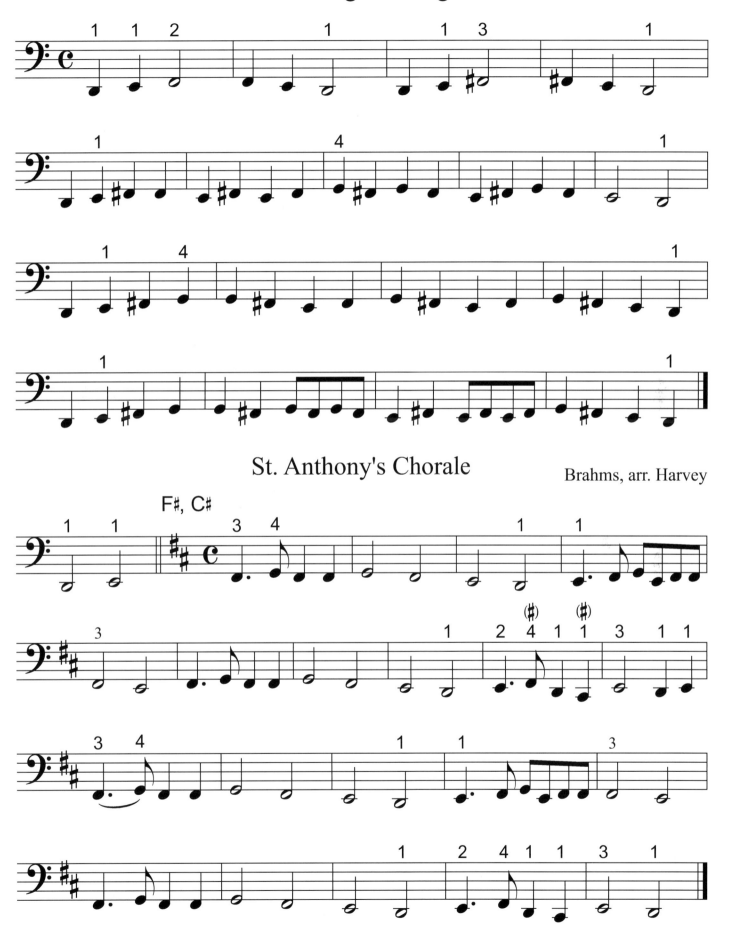

St. Anthony's Chorale

Brahms, arr. Harvey

34. Shifting Between 1st and 2nd Fingers

Drink to Me Only with Thine Eyes

Trad., arr. Harvey

35. Shifting Between 1st and 4th Fingers

Planting Grass by the Riverbank

Trad., arr. Harvey

36. Shifting a Half Step to C♮

Old Joe Clark

Trad., arr. Harvey

37. Playing C and D in Second Position

Don Gato

Trad., arr. Harvey

38. Playing C, D, and E♭ in Second Position

Hassidic Song

Trad., arr. Harvey

39. A String Shifting Patterns

Fum, Fum, Fum

Trad., arr. Harvey

40. Shifting to F on the D String

A Ya Zain

Trad., arr. Harvey

41. Playing F, G, and A♭ on the D String

The Fiddler

Trad., arr. Harvey

42. D String Shifting Patterns

Variation on "The Wind"

Bb, Eb,
Ab, Db

Trad., arr. Harvey

43. Shifting to B♭ on the G String

Russian Folk Song

Trad., arr. Harvey

44. Playing B♭, C, and D♭ on the G String

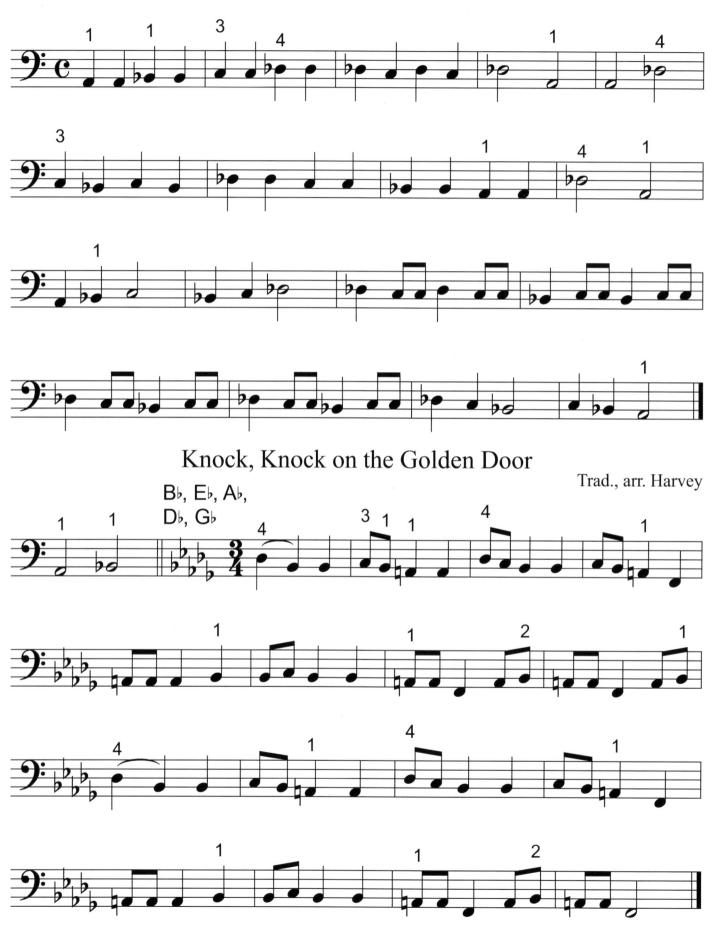

Knock, Knock on the Golden Door

Trad., arr. Harvey

B♭, E♭, A♭,
D♭, G♭

45. G String Shifting Patterns

Dos Gebel

Bb, Eb, Ab,
Db, Gb

Trad., arr. Harvey

46. Shifting to E♭ on the C String

B♭, E♭, A♭,
D♭, G♭, C♭

Magic Carpet

Harvey

47. E♭, F, and G♭ on the C String

Near the Village

B♭, E♭, A♭,
D♭, G♭, C♭

Trad., arr. Harvey

48. C String Shifting Patterns

Across the Mountains

Harvey

49. Shifting Back from 2nd Finger

Daffodils

Brockwell, arr. Harvey

50. Shifting To and From 2nd Finger

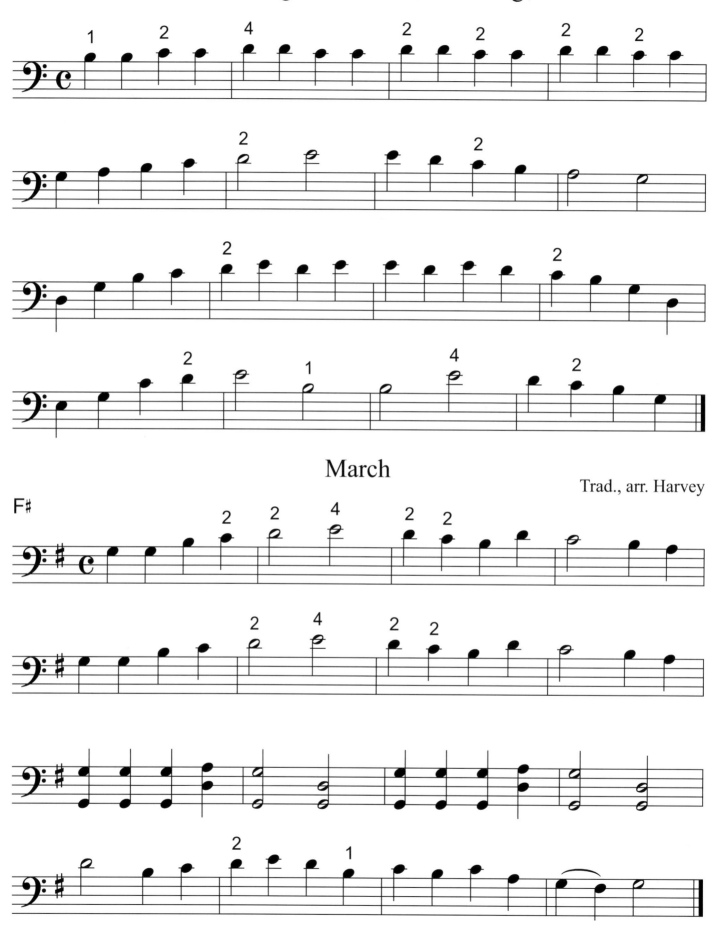

March

Trad., arr. Harvey

51. Shifting with Eighth Notes

Bartolillo

Trad., arr. Harvey

52. Maiden's Dance

Gounod, arr. Harvey

F#, C#
G#

53. Shady Grove

Trad., arr. Harvey

Go in Peace

Trad., arr. Harvey

F#, C#
G#, D#

54. Britches Full of Stitches

Trad., arr. Harvey

F#

A Silver Tapestry

Harvey

F#

A String

First Position

Second Position

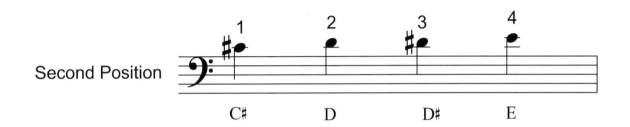

D string

First Position

Second Position

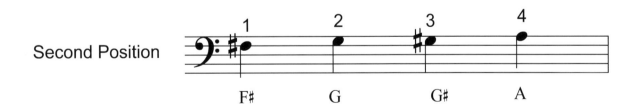

G String

First Position

Second Position

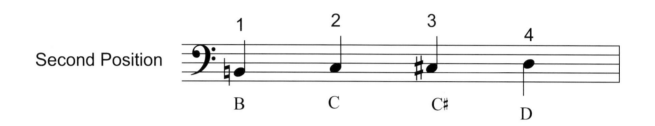

C String

First Position

Second Position

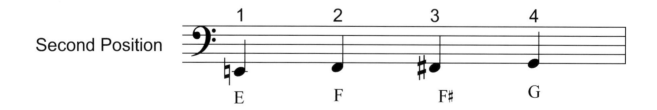

A String

First Position

Second Position

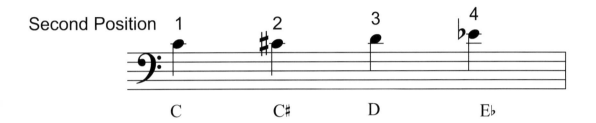

D String

First Position

Second Position

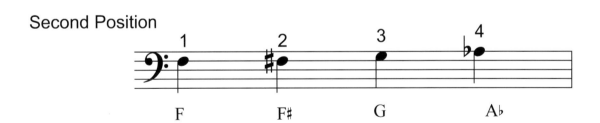

G String

First Position

Second Position

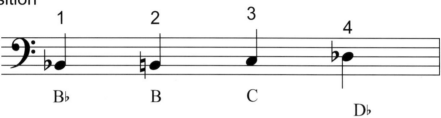

C String

First Position

Second Position

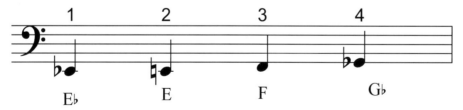

Second Position for the Cello

1

Book One

1

A string: shifting to first finger

Cassia Harvey

Ode to Joy

Beethoven